Blood Roses
He is the enemy
Somebody laughed
As she cried.
From behind, suddenly
The enemy strikes
He was speaking
Of roses, wine and life's other joys
He promised her in another life.
She is captivated
In his oceanic eyes
There lies a hidden motive.
In the darkness of the room
In the conquest of her fear
The fact this love was about to end
Somebody laughed.
All the while surrounded by roses
Clasped close to her heart.
A thorn pricks her
A drop of blood seeps
Onto the white flower.
Symbol of his conquest,
Quietly behind a hidden veil
Somebody laughed.

The Hands of Time

The Hands of Time
I lay awake each night
Hoping you will come back to me.
But you have left your body
And will forevermore soar beyond the reach of the hands of time.
Each spring that passes
Brings new life to this world
It shall never again breathe
Life into you.
Each summer brings the sun you loved so much
The pain intensifies.
The autumn brings a cool wind
I remember the last time we were to be together.
Winter with its chilling winds
Brings a closure to the day your spirit left.
Though you are not present in body,
Your spirit shall always fly through the unending hands of time.
Life was enriched because of you.
The world was a better place for it.
You left behind a legacy of love, pride and trust
Surrounded by pain.
My pain will ebb over the years
You are guiding me from immortality beyond the hands of time.
Someday I will make that journey to beyond the hands of time.
Until then I have memories to hold onto and the knowledge:
We will one day be together and
Together we will walk slowly into the hands of time.

Never Again

Never Again
Once was enough for me.
You picked up the phone to call me.
I fell for it hook, line and sinker.
This time it'll be different.
We got along great
How could things have become so bad?
When you were in love with me
And I was struggling to get out -
Never again will I go back to you.
We had our share of arguments
And our share of joy
Never again will I feel such hatred
As I did then.
My phone rang,
Such a noise,
So I picked it up only to hear you.
Never again will we be together
In time perhaps forgiveness will come,
Never again will we walk arm in arm.

Player

Player
You played me for a fool.
Thought I'd never figure it out.
Pretending you cared
When you didn't.
How could I have been so blind?
Why didn't I see it?
Could I have been so blind?
Two girls for one guy
Did she know about me?
So many unanswered questions
That I don't ever want answers to
You are such a player
I warn others about you too.
Hopefully they take my advice
And steer clear of you.

Take To The Skies
This pain is not caused by me.
I try to alleviate it, but the doctor says,
"He'll take to the skies soon.
There's nothing more we can do."
"But you have to do something!"
Nothing more.
I go to talk.
The words that once flowed so smoothly
now don't want to come.
Instead of words I feel my face moist with tears.
"I should be comforting you not this way," I say.
He says, "I am comforted in knowing
soon I'll take to the skies and will be in pain no longer."
I say that I'm selfish in wanting him to stay.
He says I'm not.
He starts to say something but his face eases into a smile and flatlines.
"Take to the skies and wait for me," I whisper.
I'll never forget you, for with your parting you take my heart.

Mental Anguish and For Dan

Mental Anguish
The pain you caused stays with me.
It will stay with me forever.
My mind will continue to put me through grief
Until I get you out of my mind
There will always be mental anguish.

For Dan
I know it's better to cry-
To let it all out.
But I'm afraid if I say what I feel
I'll be alone forever.
Crying only lessens the pain a little
I have so much to want to cry about
It's not fair how you can lead me on
Pretending like you cared.
I think you liked me for a brief time
Not so long ago
I'll always care for you
I don't think you gave a damn.

Apparition

Apparition
Once a long time ago
In another place
In another time
You appeared to me.
No one believes me,
They say I lost it
The day you left.

I know though
That it was you.
We shared a bond
That will never be broken
It was you I saw
That night
So long ago

Then I knew I had to
Carry on.
I have to live on
Until the mission
Is fulfilled.
That night
I saw an
Apparition.

They say I saw
A ghost.
Ghosts linger because
Of an unfulfilled
Mission.
How I know you were an
Apparition is

Apparition

You passed on
Your mission
To me.
I gave you
My word
My word is bond.
I swear I'll fulfill your Mission.

Vision

Vision
I had a vision of you.
Maybe it wasn't so long ago,
But it feels like eternity.

You came to me
To prove that you were safe,
In Heavens arms.

Your message was simple
To love, to assist
Be the best you can.

Why did you choose to see me?
What did I do to be so blessed?
Are you always watching me?

There are so many things
I want to ask you.
I'll have to save them for some other time.

The last time I saw you
You were not afraid
Please guide me in my decisions.

Maybe I'm losing my mind.
Maybe I'm not.
All I know

Is I saw a vision of
You in your glory,
You surrounded by a pure light

Vision

You are an angel now.
Not any angel-
My Angel
And I know in your heart

You are content in
Never growing older
And keeping me safe from harm.

Injured

Injured
I am injured
My heart is injured.
There was no way I could save myself
From the injury of rejection.
It takes so long for
An injured heart
To learn to trust
Again.
But my heart
Always gets me into
More injury each time I
Fall in love.
An injured heart
Takes so long to heal.
And by the end of my life
My heart will probably
Look like a patchwork quilt.
It is patched from all the injuries
Thank you for helping me
Get over my injuries.

Final Farewell and If Only

Final Farewell
It is time to say goodbye.
Not goodbye for eternity - for now.
As I lift a flower to my lips
I say a little prayer
Go with God.
I'll be along soon.
This is my final farewell to you on Earth.
The wet Earth is piling up.
I can no longer bear to watch.
I'll talk to you in my subconscious
Until we are together again
This is my final farewell.

If Only
If only you hadn't left
Then I wouldn't feel this way.
But since you're gone I must continue.
If only the rain didn't come down so hard.
My heart has been hit with hurricane rain.
If only the sun didn't shine so brightly
As if to mock.
If only you were still here with me.

Dependant
I can't believe
That I'm so dependant on you.
Thought I'd never lose my freedom.
I know I'm still free.
But it's like I'm not.
Through my heart and mind I am free.
And I shall always stay true
To my heart.
Now I am with you.
And my knowledge can only grow into wisdom.
One day perhaps I will
Surpass the wisdom of the elders.
But until that day
My heart will be dependant on you.

Stop

Stop
We're moving too fast
For me.
I want us to stay together
But if things stay this way
I'll have to say goodbye,
It's not what I want to do,
All I really want to tell you
Is to keep things in perspective,
We're young and have so
Much more to live for.
Try to keep things in perspective.
You're making me uncomfortable,
I know you don't realize that
But now it's time
For you to stop
And think about
The things that you have done.

Don't Leave

Don't Leave
Don't leave.
Don't walk out that door.
If you do
I just might end up
Missing you.
We shared our secrets,
Our hearts,
Stay by my side
Because if you leave
I might just end up missing you.
Don't leave
I need to hear your voice
To see your face.
Don't leave
You'll leave me broken hearted.
Do you really want to do that?
Don't leave otherwise
I just might end up
Missing you.

Don't Shed a Tear

When I leave tonight
There is but one request:
Don't shed a tear over me.
You watch me pack my bags
And put them by the door.
I look into your eyes
They are moist.
I don't want to cause
You pain but looking at your face
Don't shed a tear
Over me.
You will move on
I know that.
Get on with your life
Don't shed a tear
Over me.

Forgiveness

Forgiveness

There's one thing I need more than anything else.
That's your forgiveness.
I tried not to hurt you,
There was nothing I could do
He likes me
And I like you but I'm with him.
He treats me like a princess
I'm his royalty
You will always be in my heart
Never leaving it
I need one thing
That is to know you're not mad at me
And I need your forgiveness.
I'm not sorry
For anything I've done so far
I just want your forgiveness
To carry on.

Hey! Hey!

**Hey! Can anyone hear me?
Am I getting through?
Hey! I'm not a piece of dirt.
Hey! Listen to me.
I've got something to say
And I'm gonna say it now
Whether you hear it or you don't
That's your choice.
Hey! Hey! Why do you treat me so?
I try to be good -
I even try to love you.
Hey! You're not paying attention.
Why should I care?
I told you
I'm not a piece of dirt.
Pay attention
Hey! You only live once
I'm leaving slowly.
Hey! You don't care.
Hey! Can anyone hear me?
Hey! Listen to me.**

Expectations

Expectations
Hopes set high.
Probably too high
Maybe not high enough
Are my expectations for you.
They are right up there in the sky
It's probably because I don't know you
In fact I know it is
My expectations for you are so high
I only hope I won't be disappointed
I don't think I will be.
I hope I live up to your expectations of me.

I Care

I Care
Why should I care what
People think of me?
It's not my choice to
Have them like me or hate me.
Not my loss, not my gain.
If they don't like my
Choice not to do drugs or alcohol
So be it.
I choose not to inflict my body with pain.
I care what happens to my body, to my life.
Why should I care what
People think of me?
I have my family -
My close circle of friends
They will stand by my side
Through thick and thin.
My decisions come after long and careful thought,
Though some come in a few minutes
When I begin to feel uncomfortable
In a situation.
After I am removed and
My thoughts have had time to collect
I come to realize
My choice was the right one.

As Far As You'll Get

I don't know what the other
Girls you went out with were like.
I don't honestly care.
I care that you are with me.
How far you got with them
Is for your knowledge -
I don't want to know.
All I know is that
You've gotten as
Far as you're
Going to get
With me.
I don't know what you did to them
Or what you did with them,
But I'm not them I'm me
Don't take this wrong - I love you
Honest I do
You've gotten as far as you're
Going to get with me.
I love you - honest I do.

More Than I Can Give

More Than I Can Give

**I think you were expecting more
From me.
But I'm not ready to give more.
What you get is what you get
I believe in that after marriage.
Take what you get seriously
If you don't you'll never see me.
I mean this as truth
And I don't want to get hurt.
The best way to shield myself
From hurt is not to do that.
You were expecting more
I never thought I'd kiss you like
I have.
Take that as far as it will go
But that's all your getting from me.
I do believe I love you
If in fact I know what love is,
We are so young
And we have so much more to live for
We have to keep things in perspective.
I believe that you love me, and I love you
Know that my expectations of you were
Great and you lived up to them.
I hope I lived up to yours though I don't think
That I did because you want more
Than I can give.
You're not asking for so much
But I can't give you everything.
Be blessed that you have love
Don't push it - in time with someone else**

More Than I Can Give

You are asking for so much more
Than I can give.
It would be the same if we were older
I believe in what I say
Please don't push it
You're asking for more than I can give.

There Was / I Stayed

There Was

There was a time
I would have given it all up for you.
There was a time my heart
Sang a song of love for you.
There was a time when I would fall in love
With each word your lips spoke.
But it's not now
However know that there was.

I Stayed

I stayed when you
Said we needed space.
I stayed single in
The hope you would
Come back to me.
The hope has never left.
So I stayed
Waiting for you.
You never came to your senses
But I stayed.

I Don't Have A Role For Love

I Don't Have A Role For Love

I don't have a role for love to play in my life now
You have to understand that this is coming
From my heart and I mean it very much.
I will not get hurt, I won't let myself.
You don't understand that I have
A dream for myself that I
Must fulfill and know
No one will stand
In my way
Of my
Goal.
I don't have a role for love to play in my life now
You have to understand that this is my life
And I will not let my route become
Detoured by any trial caused
By love and my heart so
Now know that I
Am shielding
Myself of
Pain.

Not Out of My Heart

Not Out of My Heart

Gone - vanished into thin air
Hoping you will come back to me
I can still feel your hands caressing my hair.
In a way I know we will never be
Though you have left me
Tired, lonely, confused and sad
How could this be?
Never knowing I could feel this bad
All I can see is the way we had to part
You and me
You'll never be out of my heart.

Used To Be

Once there used to be
An era of respect and pride.
There once was a time
When you cared for me
And I cared for you.
But as stated before
Used to Be.
Since then the days
Go by so much slower.
The sun doesn't stay so high.
Maybe it's my
Imagination
But we once used to be.

Star Tears / Questioning

Star Tears
The stars are the tears
Shed for you.
Each tear is a memory
Memories last forever.
Crying doesn't help much
It can't bring you back
But it can release some of the pain inside.
When I'm hurt
Or upset
My last reminder of you
Comes out;
A picture-
A little treasure:
A symbol of my love for you.

Questioning
What does it mean to be here?
Do we really feel things
Or only pretend to?
Does life only last until we die
Or does it thrive eternally?
Shall our legacy
Live on
Longer than our deaths?
Questions that shall
Never die
Live on
As death lasts forever.
Does another life
Take the place of
Ours when ours is lost?

Allowing / Do Not Disturb

Allowing
You allow yourself to be controlled.
Be your own person
Stop allowing
Yourself to be
Controlled.

Do Not Disturb
Do not disturb my universe.
My universe is my soul
I cannot change.
Please take care of my
Balance - It's a delicate one.
Please do not disturb my train of
Thought because
I'm thinking of you.
My thoughts no one else could follow
Only me.
The only person who could understand
My language - my thoughts
Is me.
Do not disturb my universe.

Hold My Head

Hold My Head

**It's impossible for you to know
What you have done to me.
You don't know the love and
Hate and scorn and contempt
I feel inside.
Trying to sort out these
Emotions is an impossible task
Eternity won't be long enough.
Baby, I have to thank you
For what you've done
You've given me a reason to
Live on to prove to you
That I will go on
Without you.
That will come later
For this moment
I'm holding my head
While the tears
Just keep coming.**

Forbidden Romance

Found out
Torn in two
Life is hell
Fires burning
You can't see me
For a forbidden romance.
Parents questioning
Why oh Why
Don't you have common sense?
Yes, but.....
Stopped
All for a forbidden romance.
Do they really think that a
Determined heart
Will quit?
Finding a way out
Will be tricky
Hoping one day trust
Will one day be restored
All these repercussions
For one Forbidden Romance.

Hidden Away

Hidden Away

Can there be a way
To allow me to open this
Safe of memories?
Tucked in a dark corner
Of my heart
Hidden by a barrier
Rarely able to be seen
By anyone
It is here that the
Memories of you and I are
Tucked safe and sound
No, I have never forgotten
You. It's impossible to.
However you are
Hidden away forevermore
In a corner of my heart.

And The Tears Keep Coming

Ever since you left me
I've been alone
At night before I
Go to sleep
I say my prayers
Praying for you to come back to me
And the tears keep coming
Not ceasing for a while
I climb into bed
And pull the covers
Tight around me
As I lay my head on
My pillow a tear
Drips from my eyes
And the tears keep
Coming softly quietly
Another night when I
Cried myself to sleep.

Stupid Things

I don't know
All the reasons why
I did what I did.
I realize now all
Were stupid things
Which could have ended my life
Tragically.
I guess now
I can chalk it up to being young and stupid.
Maybe I would have
Realized it sooner
But I didn't.
I'm glad that now
I know and am able
To have people there
Step by step so that
I never do those
Stupid things
Again.

One of Those Things

That stage of my life
Is over and no matter
How bad I wish those
Years to be taken back
They can't.
Nothing could have been
Done to change my mind
It was one of those things
That simply could not have been
Stopped no matter how
Hard anyone tried.
Anyway that part of my life is
Over and there is no
Turning back.

Fall Apart

Not knowing of
The damage
That could have occurred
I persisted.
Forced to own up
To a terrible reality
I realized
One eminent thing
Nothingness if it
Continued.
My life would have fallen apart
But it didn't.

Down In Hell

Barren wastelands
Cruel sun
Me, lying abandoned
Helpless to the fury
The winds whip
Stinging my skin
Yet I'm numb to the sense
Screaming - answered
By only silence.
Void where vibrancy
Should be.
Deaf, mute, and blind
To surroundings
Me, in my vast desert
Praying for darkness
To encircle me.

Prayer of the Dying

**Alone, wandering
Drifting farther and farther
No one understands
Nor seems to care
Said she's to young
Too full of promise
What a waste life is.
Nothing more to live for
Wanting to be free
Only death can
Let her be.
Was there something
That could have been done to
Save her they will ask
Yes! screams her spirit
Alas, in death's cold clasp
Her voice is muted
She wants to tell them
Just listen, it may seem
Childish and unimportant to you
But to her it is important
See what you have done she cries
A tear from her mothers grief stricken face
The coffin closes.**

Do You Know Me?

Do You Know Me?

**No way to perfection
She cries in the night
Slowly wearing herself
To nothingness.
Her life is a tailspin
Headed for a fall
She controls but one thing
Her appetite.
For life it has not diminished
For the spirit soars
For the future it shakes
For food no more.
She's no where near perfection
She won't ever be
Can't they just see
All she wants is to be free?
If freeing herself is
By means best left unsaid
She just might be willing to
Take that risk
Better watch how you step.**

Only Happiness

I never thought I
Could say these words
To you.
I cared and still care
In my own silly way
You and I shared a
Moment however fleeting
As fast as it came upon us
It disappeared
and was gone.
We have both
Moved on into
A new world
Where neither one is a part of the others
For all the things
We have shared
I don't want you
To regret the time with me.
I know I could never
Regret devoting myself to you
When you think of me do not be sad
Because when I think of you
Only happiness comes to mind.
And as our worlds grow farther apart
With each new person
New experience
You are a part of my heart Always.
You are my best friend
I am always here for you
And now you have met
Someone else - I hope

That she brings only
Happiness to you.

An Endless River

Once a long time ago you
Asked how many tears does
It take to make an ocean?
Now I can answer
I know now
And it's thanks to you that
I do.
Baby you broke my heart
I gave you everything and more
I let you into the deepest
Corners of my heart and you
Robbed me of my ability to trust.
Now I'm crying an endless river
Didn't think I could cry this much
Thought I had protected myself
From something like this
But baby you passed through the barrier
And got into my heart
Once when my heart screamed out for your name
Just the thought was enough to make me
Smile.
Now is no longer
I'm screaming in pain,
And needing you all the more
But baby our plans
Once fertile as the rainforest
Also as dense
Now barren
And alone
As the desert
Also as parched.

Time Wears On
I’ve known fear
I’ve loved and lost
Then gained the courage
To love again.

Losing
Flowers bloom
Flowers die
Life ends like a dream
Someday they end like a light beam
Probably won’t go to the sky
Why the hell even try?

Not Who I Seem

Hopeless
Empty in the soul
Alone
Wandering
Needing so much more
Not what I bargained for
Cold steel
Sharpened to perfection
Ready to be embedded
Deep into the soul
Of me.
Past the flesh
Through the bone
Driven by voices
Driven home.

Guiltiest Of Eyes

Guiltiest Of Eyes

It's the saddest of eyes
That shed the most heart wrenching cries
They condemn the man who dies
Those guiltiest of eyes.

It's the crack dealer selling on the street
But it's the mother who pays when her child's carried out by the feet.
It's the reporter itching for a burning story
Does anyone truly receive glory?
For the child who saw horrors in the day
And at night it's the parent who turns them away
It's the adventurous one who wants to talk the dare
Put the blame on those who said thcy didn't care.

It's the weariest of souls
Who see all of societies holes
Who condemns the society of crime that thrives?
Those guiltiest of eyes.

He with ravages of war, remember where the broken bodies lie
Walk away, come back, see them die.
Who pays the price of that age old politics game?
They who are immobile, cripple and lame.
Who are the children's role models?

Many are those whose lives are consumed in bottles.
Say I'm sorry for driving with excess speed
Won't do a bit of difference to those lives lost without need.

Guiltiest Of Eyes

It takes the guiltiest of eyes
To overlook the lies
It takes the guiltiest soul
To do nothing on society as a whole
Where do we all fit?
Where do I fit?
How many mothers have cried

Cause their child's watching from the skies
Killed by the guiltiest of eyes.

Lines

Lines

You haven’t called
So it’s over
Don’t want it to be
But this time the choice wasn’t up to me
I saw the end of the road coming
Didn’t need any fancy signs
All I did was read between the lines.
Those curt conversations
No more affection
All I did was read between the lines.

Grieve

**In this world of ours
Media's got all the power
To control all we see
Are we really free?
Can we really block out bad things
And keep those secret dreams?
I grieve for the children of tomorrow
I can already feel their sorrow
I grieve for the honest worker
Who's fired because of some merger.
I grieve for the students plight
It's gonna take all their strength to fight.
Can this world get any better?
We can make a difference with just one letter
So many people vying for power
No wonder corporations grow sour
Nuclear weapons oozing
Does anyone really know what they're doing?
I grieve for all of the future
Let the present be their tutor
I grieve for the past
They thought ideas and morals would last
I grieve for those this world has charmed
Reality is they're not welcomed opened armed
Society affects us all
We have to stand brave and tall
Unite into one power
Standing till our final hour
Absolving each and every sin
Is the only way we just might win
I grieve for my future children**

Grieve

There'll be no parks for them to play in
I grieve with those who mourn
Looking at society with scorn
I grieve with those emotions I have felt
We have to play the hand that we've been dealt.
I grieve.

Waves

**The waves lap gently at my feet
Beckoning me to join
They rush cool water between my toes
And I look up at you and we laugh
Dancing together to our own melody
The moon our spotlight
We have the entire floor
As we collapse breathless in
Each others arms
Couldn't help but notice
Our song was fading
With each passing wave
So this time we danced
Slower and closer
Leaving a deep impression
In the sand and my heart.
The steps will fade
The memory grow fuzzy
Yet we will be tied together
For the waves.**

Treasures Grove

The world surrounding
Hot, muggy, humid
Reeking with the stench
Of day old food
Lost will to exist
I remember the days
We'd spend laying under the shade
Of that huge oak tree
Remember how the dew
Would soak your shirt
And dry slowly
Refreshing you?
I recall running the
Damp grass having it
Tickle the bottoms of my
Feet. Then you would
Twirl me in mid air
Holding me so I couldn't fall
Then sitting having
Ice cold lemonade
Holding your hand
Down in that place of ours.
I went back there
The other day, you know;
Physically you weren't there
In my heart you were
And I ran, and I ran
Running breathless to the wind
Recollecting every past emotion
Every memory
Then I collapsed under that

Treasures Grove

Big oak tree
Closed my eyes picturing
You sitting next to me.
I needed you then
As I still need you now
And this time I know
You want and need me too
For our times in the grove
You've given me so much
To live for
You've given me the treasure grove.

Mistakes of Cowardice

It was all my fault
Put the blame on my shoulders
I was so afraid of losing
I drove you away my love.
Didn't want what happened
With him and me to become
A repeat this time through
You and me.
Because I was scared and scarred
Crucified but not yet delivered
I drove you away
Left my arms empty,
Left me to dwell in my thoughts
I'm not a survivor
I'm not a victim
All I have is a yellow spine.

Kiss
Set up by a family friend
Who thought that we would
Make a cute couple.
We never "dated"
Go out, hang out, yes
Date, no.
Always ended in a hug
But never for long
Some thing more meaningful
Than this
All only one
Kiss.

Trapped
No one can hear her
She's screaming at the top of her lungs.
In the middle of this crowded room
No one wants to take responsibility
For her, this wisp of a person
Where the reason and hope are
Is where she longs to be
She longs for a freedom
That can never be.
A freedom which she can never live.

Made Me Happy

That short time you and I
Were together, not so long ago
Was the best time I'd
Ever spent.
You made me happy
When I felt as if I could not
Go on any longer
It was you who lifted me
Above my pain and sorrows
Gave me a reason to
Look forward to the tomorrows
You made me happy.
I'm not the person you
Once knew me to be
I've grown up
Developed my personality
And have never - nor will I ever
Let you out of my heart.

Clip My Wings

Said love is blind
Said you could say anything on your mind
But I was never in love
Never cared for you
All you did was put me down
No compliments
You're too fat
You're hairs too long
I'm not perfect
But you don't have to point
Out all my flaws
You wanted to make me a Barbie
Put me on a stand for display
Your vision of who and what
I should be
As I told you time and time again
Don't clip my wings
I'll flinch and die
I need to be free
Not caged up in a pen
On display for the world to see
So I flew away
I was never 'with you'
Yet you tried to own me.

What's Gone
I miss you
Haven't seen you in so long
At least one month.
We talk every night
And talk about what's gone.
The time is lost to us forever
It can never be given
To us again.
What's gone is those hours
We could have spent together
But you and I are
In love.

Dreams
I guess by now the dream is over
You remember, the one we dreamed together
The one where the world
Would accept us for us
And not mind the differences in our ages.
It's probable that it started
So many moons ago
With the discontent of my parents
Yet we persisted.
We lasted so long together as a couple
But we drifted apart
Not for any factor regarding age.
We became much closer soon after
And are back together stronger than ever.
I love you with every ounce of my being.
That dream of acceptance is gong
You and I will survive somehow.

Insomnia

**Every night I'm just
Tossing and turning
In my bed.
So lonely without you
The clock refuses to change
It's been an hour - actually a minute
I've lain here.
Needless to say time is slow
Drags on for days on end
And there's no way to
Exit.**

Dreaming Again

**Another lost chance to love
Gone tonight with
One blink of an eye.
You say that you love me
Only want me to be with.
Total chaos surrounding us
Needing to be with you
More than anything else
Nothing but you by my
Side matters at all.
Shelter me from every peril
Give me strength to face
My darkest hour
Let me love you now.**

A Dying Dream

Fearing persecution by the people
Those who care least about me
Hold the keys to the rest of my life.
I cannot die, not me not now
Not here.
This can't be happening to me
I'm being taken over
Forced into the corner by the shadows
Looking at my life
Realizing it's such a waste
Fallen barren to the hard ground
Seeing my dying dream.
Knowing it is all that is left
For me to carry on with
Searching for reason;
Logic; Power a part of me
Like life support I cling to it.
Only to watch the
Beautiful painted picture of life
Melt away into the darkness
Of death.
My dying dream - a prayer
A piece of my soul
The story of life.

Shadow

I thought that we had been given
A second chance to be together.
All went smoothly
As on a newly paved road
But, just like last time
One bump and
It all fell apart.
The sky turned grey
Cast a lonely shadow
On the ground.
Pointing to a different
Path - way of life.
You were my first "puppy love"
Maybe it was just infatuation
Despite the two tries we gave
That relationship I suppose
We were never meant to be.
However you have impacted
Me and my life,
The way I live
Forever.
I can promise
That you will never
Leave my heart
Just fade ever so slowly
Into the background.

Wings

I am free
With my own mind, body and soul.
You called me an Angel
Said I had a
Halo of radiant gold
And sparkling wings.
You tried to make me
Stay with you.
Tried to change the me inside
To suit you.
Tried to clip these
“Heavenly wings” so I
Would never fly from
Your side
That was the biggest
Mistake you ever could have made.
Let me live
Don’t drag me down
Allow me to thrive
Don’t kill my reasons for live
You cared for me
This I know.
And if you care about someone
You’ll set them free
Not clip their wings
Allow them to fly to the Heavens
And live.

Turn To Cry

Ever since you left me here all alone
I've cried the river Nile.
Just can't seem to stop the tears from streaming down my face.
This isn't fair what you're doing to me
Ohh baby I don't need another turn to cry
What you give is what you get
I'll be over you so quick
Soon you'll realize what a prize you had
And I'll be laughing cause
It's your turn to cry
You tried to bring me down but I pulled myself back up
I wasn't for falling.
Guess at first it was infatuation
Cause true love
Could never feel like this
ooohhh
It's not my turn to cry
I can't even fake a tear when you're here
Just want to leave and let you see
What a chance you had with me
I won't be stepped on
Won't be let down
Cause of you
Cry over me.
Now you'll know what it feels like
Cry over me.
Cry
Cry, Cry

Chameleon

I found out
Six months ago
Another color
Another violent side.
You changed ever so gracefully
At the drop of a hat
The drop of a tear.
You pretended to care
When all you wanted
Was control over me.
Treated me like a possession
Rather than a person
Wanted to make me over
Just so you could be
Happy and contented.
It wasn't me
And I had never seen
This side of you before.
Thought you were decent
And thought you cared
But you abused me and beat me
Causing pain and more stress
Than I deserve.
How fickle!
What a character!
Changing colors constantly!

No Boundaries

I'm praying for that day
The day when the world will know about us
When we will be accepted for what we are
Where no one will degrade or put down
Can't they just see we have feelings too?
We were willing to take a chance
On each other
Probe into emotions and soul
Really get to know
And once we saw we had that spark
Waited for the fire inside to start
Burning bright.
We're still waiting for that day
When there will be no boundaries
Placed on us
And we will be judged
Only by our love.

Break Your Heart

**Those things you heard
About me breaking guys hearts
That's all true.
It's so hard to stay with someone
Who attaches himself and holds on tight
Sweetheart, I've never been one to
Say my feelings out loud
But if you stay with me
I'll never break your heart
Listen to me - I'm begging you
Not to leave
Never did this before
Can't believe my voice
Is forming these words
My hand writing them
I love you too much
To ever hurt you.
Never will I consider
Breaking your heart.
Fall in love with me
As I have with you
And just never break
My heart.**

Screaming Your Name

**It is never easy to see you go
I want to spend every
Waking second with you.
Though that is impossible
We are connected at night
Through dreams.
Mine are of you
And I wake up
Screaming your name
Alone and scared
Without you near
Everything frightens me
You are a security blanket
One that I won't outgrow
Until you can be with me
I'll wake up each
And every morning
Screaming your name.**

All Over Again

**So I was a mistake
You never expected
To like me so much
So soon anyway.
I came to you quickly
Or as you put it:
"A thief in the night
Who stole my heart."
I didn't mean for that
Besides, we were over
As soon as we'd even begun
I know you were
Good to me and
Good for me.
In one heartbeat
I'd do it all over again
You and I together
Were something special;
We complimented each other
So perfectly
I know we rarely talk now
And for that I'm sorry
We had a great friendship going
It's a shame to lose it all
But there is one last
Question inflicting my mine
I know that I would do it all
Over again.
But would you?**

As I Wander

As I wander this lonely road
Searching for my truth
My way to love.
Hoping it will come upon me
As a vision in the night
Leading me to hope
Guiding me to love
The winds pick up
I pull the jacket tighter
Around me
Trying to keep in the
Warmth so desperately
But here my solitary figure
Stands in puzzlement
Contemplating her fate
Feeling condemned to loneliness
For the rest of her life.
Dreading the eternity
Of love without a truth
Of a commitment that
He will not stay
That he is going to
Leave without love.

You Miss Me

Breaking apart
Patching pieces
Mending hearts
Getting together
Learning love
Piece by piece
Little by little
When we part
Do I have to
Deal with the
Pain once again?
Do I have to
Deal with consequences?
Why let you free
Cause of my fragile
Condition once before
Almost my death
Later I trusted
Once again.

Kindness

Joy will come
Again to me
Of this I'm sure.
Where once there
Was a pitiful and
Wretched life there is
Now hope.
Her life had been
A downward spiral
Going out of control
But with the help
Of one special friend
And the kindness
That only he could
Bring to her
She left the
Helplessness to make
A new life

Time To Move On

We have not been
A couple for eight months.
Don't you think it is
Time for you to move on?
You're obsessing over me
And the truth is
You're scaring me greatly.
Please move on with your life
Get a new girlfriend.
I can't be yours again
Once was enough for me
But more importantly
I'm involved in a relationship
At this current time.
He is everything I want
I'm completely over you
I think it's pointless to say
That you should realize it's
Time to move on.
Put the past behind you
Let go of me - I've
Flown away a long time ago.
You didn't realize what
You had way back when
And now you realized your
Mistakes. But I'm not
Yours to have.
I think it's time for you
To move on.

Face To Face

Break up with me
In person.
Not over the phone
Or letter
Or through a friend
Or through an e-mail.
Be the man you are supposed
To be - the man
Everyone says you are.
Personally I don't see it.
You haven't been so
Up front with me
Please give me some
Dignity let me keep some.
I know this has been coming
For some time now.
I think you knew
It too.
We're not working out
I do honestly love you and
I suppose that I always will.
Watch as the tears stream
Down my face.
Don't pretend you're not
Feeling any emotions,
Because I know you better
Than that.

Hate

The rain is pouring down around me
In torrents.
Engulfing me, overpowering me.
Lifting my face
Welcoming the torment of the storm
Beating in anger
Suppressing the hatred
I feel inside of me.
The friends once held so dear
Now are no longer.
Looking in a mirror
Gazing at the emaciated figure
Staring back with hollow eyes
Wan and restless
A child-like creature
A haggard old woman
Beat up by emotions
Raped by time
Life is an illusion
No key to any trick
Can solve it.

Questions

Do you love me?
Do you need me?
Do you want me?
Do you want me as your wife?
Have you been hurt before?
Do you think that I'll hurt you?
Do you dream of me every night?
Are you just fooling around with me?
Is there someone else?
Do you love her?
Do you even like me?
Do you want to be only friends?
Do you want to talk to me?
Do you want to hold me?
Do you want to kiss me?
Do you want to love me?
Do you want me to love you?

Shut Out

**Is there something wrong with me?
Did I do something to hurt you?
Is there another girl?
I feel so shut out of
Your world
Every time I call you
It seems you just brush
Me aside and I want
To know the hidden truth.
Open the doors to me
Like tonight you were so curt
And I couldn't think that
You have shut me out of
Your life forever.**

Live On

You are safe in
My being.
I'll never let go of you.
Though we have been
Separated by uncontrollable forces
We cling together
As long as I live
You too will live on
Existing only in my memory.
I have a few pictures
Momento's to remember you by
But as long as I have my
Memory you will live on.
And when the time comes to
Join you once again
We shall live out eternity together.
And our memory will be
Imprinted in the minds of
Those our lives have impacted.

Rain

She is hurt
Because he
Did not call tonight.
She fears her choice
Has made him leave.
Did she do the right thing?
Her conscience is her answer
She must answer to herself
Above all - no one else.
Before she chose
He said he would think more of her
Now it seems as if
The rain cloud is pouring
All the world's sorrows
Upon her.
So young to handle
Such major responsibilities
She chose
Here are
The consequences.

Flower

Her innocence has been lost
Such a long time ago
She feels no emotion
No remorse
No love.
She has been hurt
A thousand times before
Nothing can repair
The damage done.
She is the precious baby
Who is a baby no longer
But a woman
Forced to make her
Own choices and
Forced to pay the consequences.
She has grown up
Matured overnight
Blossomed brightly as a flower
Until all that is left
For her is to wilt.

Holding My Pillow

How I wish you
Were here tonight.
But you are not
For reasons beyond
Your control
So I'm left
Here alone
Holding my pillow
Wishing it were you
Pulling it tighter
I close my eyes
And dream of you
And me together
Hoping that when
I open my eyes
The pillow will be
Replaced by you.
But it isn't.
I'm still holding
My pillow
Wishing it was you.

Cease

Darkness has come
The company is gone
Alone she stands.
Tears streaming down her
Dirty face
Leaving those years behind
Walking to the kitchen
Looking at the glistening blade
End it all a voice tells her
Yet another says live.
She wonders what friends and family
Would say if
She ceased to be.

Fiery

Help me
Drowning in a sea
Of useless words
Being hung in a noose
With each action
Caught on fire
Burning alive
Seething in rage
Pent up anger
Shot in the heart
Slowly dying
Life leaking slowly
From my body
Pallid tone to
Grey hue
Drained life
Seeping between
My fingers
No more air
Gasping but
Alas.

A World Away

Time and distance
No longer matter.
Life has left your body
Stranded me desolate, alone.
As the tears stream down
My face,
Whispered to the winds
To come and set me free.
Free of the oppression
Of the bonds within.
Believing you are not gone,
You are still here with me.
Watching me.
Guiding me.
Protecting me.
Loving me.

Unconditionally

To dance
As in a dream
I am no longer alone.
Through the night you come to me
See me awaken
To your touch.
I arise to dance with you.
Into the night our dance:
Our passion
Carries forth unto a new day
The dance overpowers me
And I succumb to the force
The shining lights:
The love of our lives
Created by this dance
The dance of life
We dance well into the night
Allow nothing to separate us
Under the light of
The stars in the sky
Your senses sharpen
And begin to feel
Dawn approached
And begins to wake me
Until tonight my love
You and I shall dance
The dance of love.

Angel Falling

Light beams down through the night
On a young girl brushing her flaxen hair.
Everything seems so right.
But take a good look at her she's awfully fair.
You see death when you look at her
No one is left to hold her hand
Perhaps her next birthday gift will be myrrh
Death has the strongest demand
It surrounds her in every way
To her it seems
She might not see another day
Only to live in a dream.
Barely allowing herself to hope
Never uttering a sound
Wishing that she could cope
So she won't ever be found
Yet, in those eyes
It might have been said latter
There is something no one could despise
The hope she might one day matter.

Fear

Helpless to life
Left tattered, torn, abused
Thrown aside
Finding no reason to be in love.
No reason to live.
For what is life
Without love?
A vacuum in which
A spiral slowly
Pulls harder and stronger
Till the current overwhelms you;
Becomes you.
Spinning faster
Headfirst
Being pushed
Thrown to the bottom
The bones around you now
Remnants of the past.

Ditto

Not so long ago
I was yours
And you were mine.
Though we have
Ended the boy-friend
Girl-friend part of our
Relationship, we remain
The closest of friends.
I understood why and when
You wanted to break up
With me - the circumstances
Were right.
You were hurting and so was I.
Comfort can only come from within.
I can't quite recall it -
Just how you put it
You said you wanted to be
My best friend
Until the end of time
With the tears streaming
Down my face
You urging me not to cry
Slowly I replied.
Weak at first then
Much louder, stronger
Confident I raised my eyes
And said:
"Ditto."

I'll Never Stop Loving You

**When I needed you
So long ago
You were there for me
Devoting yourself to
My every beck and command
You were there for me
By my side all day
Holding my hand
Supporting me;
Carrying me when I
Could not walk.
And loving me no
Matter what I did.
You loved me
Though a trying time.
And you stuck by me
As I changed slowly.
Growing farther apart
From you until I barely
Recognize you and I also
Barely recognize myself.
Looking in the mirror
Seeing a stranger looking back
At me, but in her eyes
She realizes one thing
Has not changed in her
Life. Gone is the stranger
Replaced my her old self.
She realizes - I am back.
And no matter what I do
In life I'll never stop
Loving you.**

I'll Never Stop Loving You

That is my promise to you.

Falling

This isn't me
I see in the mirror
Everyday.
I don't know who she is
She looks so much like
A fallen angel.
There is so much that
She has done
And seen which her
Parents don't know about.
I don't know her.
She goes around
Sneaking about
Without anyone knowing
She's [I'm] like a
Falling angel.
Never thought there could
Be someone to make me
Do the things I do
Deceit, a web of lies,
She's the prey caught in the middle
And he's the spider
Who wraps her in fine silk.
Yet doesn't hurt her.
He is the gravity which
Made her fall from the
Sky into his arms.

Deepest Thoughts

**Cluttered full of cobwebs
Needing to be cleaned
Out with the old
In with the new.
Locked away in a
Hidden reach they lay
Cold as a corpse
Vast as the Earth
They are there
All on a different topic
People perhaps or even
Animals.
Guidelines also known as
Instinct a way to live.
Kept out of view
In a locked box
With a hidden key
Only needing to expose
Themselves once a lifetime.
As guides to the
Morality for life
Finding a way
Leading towards a new life.**

Reality

Just one touch from you
Sears into my skin.
It singes my hair
I'm burning
Lying crumpled in a heap
Crying lonely confused
Abandoned on your bedroom floor
Just used.
At the time it seemed
The perfect thing to do
The crux of my love for you
Now I see
The rose colored glasses
Have been lifted
All is so clear now
Used to get where you
Wanted and what you wanted
You rush to assure me
I was not used
Don't lie to me
I know I was
Leave me in peace now
Let me ponder my
Ignorance.

A Fleeting Moment

Incited by passion
Leaving dying embers
No logs left to add
Choosing to die with the fire
Leaving alone stranded
On this island
A place of no return
Stolen.
Robbed in the night
Innocence shattered
Where is he?
Gone on to
Someone new
Leaving trash
A wake of destruction
A deluge of tears.

You Long

We have had our disagreements
Had our share of sorrow.
Time didn't allow us to
Be together for that long
And now I hear how you long
For me.
Distance played a role in
Our demise, however
That was not the only factor.
We both have our faults
Not denying that.
Through the central gossip I hear
How you long to hear my voice
Touch my lips
Run your fingers through my hair.
All of these things you long for
Petitioned for and left
Unanswered.
Please with my heart and soul
I'm begging you not
To pine for me
Move on, carry forward
Live life to its fullest.

It Wouldn't Last

They said the time
Has come for us to
Start again.
We've been through break ups;
Been down the rocky road
Hit bumps and pot holes
Thrown from the car
Head over feet spiraling
Every which way head under
Toppling
Finally standing on my own
Two feet
Realizing my time with you
Is done.
Standing alone and
Loving every minute of it
Thinking out loud
Ending a relationship barely
Begun yet suddenly over
Weeping for a love that
Could have been
Yet was not nor ever was
Meant to be.
I was not made for you
We were two pieces of a puzzle
That could not fit.

Leap Of Faith

Sheltering skies
Questioning eyes
Rhythmic heartbeat
Lulling into peaceful nocturne
Gently rising
Slowly falling
Placid as the ocean
Protective yet sincere
Serene and tranquil
Tragic as innocence
Has been lost
Eyes open wide
To the world
Relishing in this
Ultimate glory.

Slipped Through the Cracks

As the sun rises
As a silent god watching it's creation
The fiery glow
Illuminated the sand in my hands.
Heaped high it trickles
Slowly yet steadily
To the ground.
The space cannot hold everything
As each grain of sand
Is something of value
In my heart.
Mid-day and my life is half over.
Only a few good things remain.
Still they trickle slowly out
Sunset comes
With wild abandon
Scratches until I resist no more.
With the fading sun
My light
Leaves and darkness surrounds
Trying to be a decent person
Living life to its fullest
Life has slipped through the cracks
And left me stranded
Alone.

Lies

Was everything you ever told me
The truth or a lie?
Did you really mean it
When you said that you loved me?
Why would you say something
Without meaning it?
After you acted was it then
You began to think of the consequences?
When I speak I say the truth
Did you?
Do you?
Is every word muttered from your lips
A lie or the truth?

What Do You See?

Included on this journey was loose soul
She wore garb of loose fitted, thrifty, handmade, beads.
Her home, like her, a dirty cramped hole.
She knew that her senses were not with deeds.
Patched, sewn, ragged, alone, hopeful, depressed
Hooked on a downward way of life by thugs
Barefoot, homeless, totally utterly stressed.
Oh, by the way she takes mind altering drugs.
Kicked out of her home by her father
Felt she could live life all on her own
He said her ideas were radical - a bother
Possibly so if you can consider cardboard a home.
Though tired, hungry, pale and terribly thin
No one holding her delicate, frail, dirty hand.
She convinces herself one day she just might win.
Slowly she walks on her journey to the promised land.

What I Don't Have
Being used
By him
Using him
Feeling lower than
The lowest scum.
Wanting to crawl
Under a rock and hide
It took so long for her
To come out of her shell
Back into her protection
Not wanting to be taken
Advantage of
Simply wanting to be
Loved.

Do You See Me?
So much to live for
Wanting to end it all
She thinks that she may be
Better off alone.
Too many people played her for a fool
Learned her lesson well
Took it to heart
Maybe to her old ways
She'll revert.
It's a warning sign
To all those that care
Damn few she notices
And proceeds slowly on.

The Past Is Never Far

Look at me
Can't you see
How I'm hurting?
Too reflect on what
I once had
And will never
Have again.
You try to enter back
Into my life yet
I am unwilling
To let you back in.
And you should
Understand that if
You want me back
You had your chance
But please
Keep our memories
Closet ridden the photo album
Will keep us together so
Remember that the past
Is never far.
And the time that we
Spent together is not
Just past. It is
Us. To see us
The past is never far.

Still There
A little bit older
A little bit wiser
Being lead by me head,
Reasoning with my heart,
Refusing to change for anyone but me
Believe me
You've got a special place
Always in my heart.

*****!
Love lost
Beliefs pulled apart
Separated into two
Reasoning no longer
Handing over our hearts
To each other
And then my
Belief in love
diminished into
Nothingness.
All the tenderness in the
World which we once shared
Not so long ago
Trying to remain as
Friends forevermore
And then leaning
More towards love
Than hate.

A Second Chance
Life is precious
Don't take that chance away
You were given a gift
A second chance,
Not only at life
But also at love.
There will be people
You will hold dear
And those that frustrate you
You were given a second chance
Please, I'm begging you
Don't waste it.

Conformity
Morals of my parents
Your morals
My morals
I have to fit the mold
I must conform
Showing you the true me
Hoping you like what you see
Believe I will change
For me and only me
You cannot force me to be
The angel of your dreams
All I can be is me
I'll adapt.

Through My Eyes

Through my eyes
You see a stranger
Looking back at you.
Now you know what I'm feeling
So abandoned and alone
Without you caring for me
I fall apart.
You look through my eyes
And see how you have treated me
I'm begging you
Please stay with me
Do not leave
Just love me
I know you love me
Just prove it.
Baby, I'm praying that you see through
My eyes and love me always.

Not Now

It can't be happening
Not to me
Not now
I promised you
I'd never hurt you
They never promised
They hurt you.
My heart is being ripped in two
Two different sides
Vying for my attention
Not now - I can't be pulled like this
Not between the two people that
Matter most to me.

Trying
Baby, don't you see we've outgrown each other?
How can you say you don't see it?
Now I'm standing at the door
Trying so desperately to catch one last glimpse of you
Watching you
Watching me
I see the world as in a dream.
Shattering silence
Broken by nothing
Don't cry my darling
No longer can we be as one
Dying to know what this end is
Hoping it's near
Begging for dear life.

Innocence Deterred
A kiss stuck in here
A look fit in so perfectly there
Walks lasting an eternity.
Feeling as high as a bird can fly
Sitting in the shade among the trees
In a secluded spot
Trying to take advantage
It's over.

Maybe / Screaming

Maybe
Maybe I am young
Maybe I am trusting
Minutes without you feel like days
Moments spent with you are so precious and rare
Maybe you are my blessing outright
Wanting to be with you for all time
Knowing I can't.

Screaming
Sail away
Leave me now.
You've caused nothing but pain
And sorrow.
Joy will come one day
In the arms of another
Sheltering you - she won't be me
Screaming because a part of me loves you
One part always will.
Screaming because a part of me hates you
One part always will.
Being pulled in two
Trying to stay together.

So Scared to Believe
It's not you I'm afraid of
It's not me either.
All I am is scared.
Scared to believe that each word
That you mutter is true.
So young for such a
Commitment have I
Even begun life?
Yet staying true to
A belief on just words
That you mutter.
Not knowing if such a
Thing as true love exists
So scared to believe you.
Not knowing if such a thing
As being a true companion
Really means faithfulness
So scared to believe you
Yet knowing that
I always will.

Torn
You both have me in a position
That I see no easy way out of.
I am torn with a choice.
If I make the wrong
Choice, what will
Happen is
Uncertain.

Each Tear Drop / Goodbye

Each Tear Drop
A trickle leaks slowly from my eye.
Warm, slightly soothing leaving a streak
Slowly opening my mind to each minute detail
Praying silently for someone to relieve the pain.
Another tear falls, then another
Soon they are falling like the rain.
With each tear that falls wipes away the fear inside
Each tear reminds me of those I'd loved and lost.
Each tear reminds me of how precious and fragile life is.
Life continues.
Slowly I lift my head and take a step forward.
It is time to move on
But I shall never forget each tear drop
And the love you left me with.

Goodbye
An ending is an ending
No matter how it is said:
"Goodbye"
"Maybe it's best if we were friends"
"We'll always be friends"
I'll have to have you leave
I don't want my heart to break
So I know I have to tell you
Goodbye.

Mean What You Say
Mean what you say
Say what you mean.
Don't lie and don't pretend
They only cause two lovers
To break apart
And lose trust in the other.
Lack of trust is a factor in
Breaking up.
Mean what you say
Say what you mean
That way the pain will last
For a shorter time.

Guilt
I feel guilty
Yet I know I should move on
You wouldn't have wanted it any other way.
We've both moved on
In our own separate ways
Maybe I should tell you
I dream about you still,
Though I've progressed on
Guilt gets the better part of my mind.
I feel as though I'm abandoning you,
I don't want to.
But I'm here without you
And I feel the way I did with you,
Except now it's him.
I guess love can be a blessing
And I was blessed
Because your love has blessed me.

Never Pretend
Don't ever pretend you feel one way
When you feel the opposite.
People get lead on and then there
Is so much hurt and lack of trust.
Never pretend you care for someone
When in reality you don't.
That only leads to heartbreak.
Never pretend to love someone
When that's not true.
Never whisper, "I love you"
To someone you don't love.
Never pretend that your feelings are
One way.
Say what you mean and don't pretend
To like what you say if you don't.

A Second In Time
It was such a long time
Ago that it happened
I can't believe how much
I've grown in that second in
Time.
That second has changed
My life in ways that no one
Could ever understand.
I can't believe that this is me
I would not think that I was this
Mature but I guess it is me.
That second in time has
Changed me forever.

Not Without A Good Fight
Every breath I take
I fight for.
Every step I take
I fight for.
Nothing comes easily
And I'm not giving anything
Up without a good fight.
I worked so hard to get to where
I am.
In my heart that's all that
Matters.
To me I have to be a
Fighter in order to survive.
Life is not always easy and smooth.
I have to fight to get to
Where I want to go.
Nothing I can see in my dreams
Will escape from me
Not without a good fight.

Forgive-Forget
Loneliness in my heart
Deepened because of why we had to part
Blame it all on me
Let me be.
Forgive me
Take me back
Forget me; Let me down so easily.
Screaming in silence
Feeling no pain
Wanting to die here
Believing there's a knife in my heart.

Mental Torture / Abandoned

Mental Torture
Medieval torture was pure torture.
I don't think it was half as harsh as you
Are putting my mind through.
You take life and me
As a joke,
Life is something for you
To map out your plan on
And I was supposed to be a pawn.
Life to you is a game
And girls are pawns
You have no clue
What a torture
You're putting me through.

Abandoned
I feel abandoned by everything and everyone
That is important to me.
I feel so alone and
I feel that no one cares what
Happens to me.
I feel that I am alone on
The road of life.
I try to get on the best that I can
But no one seems to understand
Me or my beliefs.
I don't think I'm a bad
Person
So I don't know why
Everyone I care
About seems to have
Abandoned me.

My Mind
My mind is a special place
Don't dare disturb it.
I wouldn't try if I were you,
You don't know what I'm like
You don't even know me.
You storm into my life
Like a tornado spinning
My mind in all different directions.
Life can be so strange
I don't need anyone messing
Up my mind.
My mind is a precious gift
From God to me
So don't mess with it.

I'll Be Seeing You
I'll be seeing you in a short while
We may have parted but we haven't
Parted forever.
I'll be seeing you because I love you.
You are my world - my life.
I live to see you each day.
I'll be seeing you soon.
I'll be seeing you because I love you.

Wanting Him / Fearing

Wanting Him
I never had him but I want him.
I want to be his one and only.
He knows nothing of my feelings for him
Probably he never will.
My heart is screaming
I am screaming in pain
The pain of knowing that I can never tell him
He is my friend
Yet I want more.
I don't think it will ever happen
I know he doesn't
Know how I feel
I'm scared that if he finds out
We'll be friends no longer.

Fearing
I dread what you're going to say.
I don't know why I feel this way I
Just do.
I fear getting caught in the crossfire
Of two people's affection.
I like the feeling of being liked.
However I fear rejection as everyone does.
It hurts to be rejected,
This I know as fact
It's happened before.
I just fear losing you
Because I care for you.

Pain

Pain
This is the only
Way I know to
Express myself totally.
My poems don't rhyme
They're not meant to.
It wasn't like me to fall in love.
I never meant to.
I'm so used to being rejected
And I'm so used to the pain
I'm used to being alone and I think that
I'll be alone forever.
You knew nothing of my past
And I didn't want you to find
Out anything.
If you must know I was
Hurt so very deeply by many people.
I try not to feel sorry for myself
I know I have it good
But I want someone to confide in
And I want someone to be there for me.
I'm so used to pain
It seems that I thrive on rejection
But, I don't.
When we were together
I felt on top of the world
A place that I'd never been before.
You made me feel like someone special
And that I was worth something to someone.
I fell in love with you
Never intending to.
I try to shield my heart from pain and hurt
But I guess it's my destiny to have pain.
Forgive me for this revelation

Pain

Even if you don't care for me the way I care for you
Please let me tell you I love you
I really do.

Emptiness In My Heart

Emptiness In My Heart
With your leaving
I feel nothing but emptiness.
My heart aches
Continually for you.
There is so much emptiness
In my heart since you
Left.
I didn't want you to go,
In fact I want you back
By my side always
But since you left
There is nothing but
Emptiness in my heart.
I couldn't believe that we
Had to say goodbye
We had just begun and
Just like that It was over.
I can't tell you how
Long and hard I cried
For you.
I hope you cried over me as
I cried for you.
You left an emptiness in my heart
That won't be filled for such
A long time.
I was so lonely before
You entered my life.
You left as soon as you had
Come and you took my
Heart with you.
You left me with nothing but
Emptiness in my heart.

See What You Want
You'll see what you want to see in me
There is nothing I can do to change that.
I'll only see what I choose to see in you.
I choose to get to know you
Inside out backwards and forwards.
You say you love me
How do I know that this is real?
I have to take a chance
I'll follow my heart and my instincts.
They have never failed me before
Why should they fail me now?
See what you want to see in me
Get to know me better
I think you'll like what you'll
Learn.

The Final Fire
The Earth is dark and dreary
Fire begins at a point in time.
First the fire is meant to symbolize
Love and the passion it has.
The final fire destroys all things
In its path.
It leaves a path of destruction as
Far as the eye can see - too bad we're gone.

Time For Truth

I believe you.
I never meant to lose my trust
Did you hear all the rumors that
I heard?
I don't know if you did
But all those rumors, in my mind,
Just couldn't all be lies -
Or could they?
Tell me what happened
I'm willing to listen
It's time for me to hear the truth
From you
I swear I'll believe you.
It's time for me to sort out the lies
And find the truth.
I couldn't believe you'd do such things
And I guess I jumped to conclusions
When you didn't mention them to me.
Now I believe they were rumors
Meant to hurt us
Which they did.
Let me tell you
I don't know how soon
I'll be forgotten to you
But you won't ever be forgotten to
Me.

So Hard To Say Goodbye

Because I love you
And you love me
We shared a special bond
That no one could replace.
Now that time has
Passed it's so
Hard for me to
Say goodbye.
I keep thinking
Of you and the
Little things
You'd do.
It's so hard
For me
To say goodbye.
Now that I
Can't ever see
You again
It's so hard for me
To say goodbye.
I can't believe that
It was only a few days
Since I'd heard your
Voice last.
Now I'll never hear it
Again.
It's so hard for me to say
Goodbye because I'll
Always love you.

A Little Bit Scared

**Despite all that is said
I'm not an adult.
No matter what I think
I'm still growing up.
A new adventure
Looms on the horizon
And I'm a little bit scared.
Trying not to show it
Fear is tucked way down deep inside
And a show is put on
One of an excited and eager adolescent
Inside there is a child
Yearning to be cradled like a baby.
And tucked into bed once more
Wishing to be sung to like
Once upon a time.
Now outwardly that child is grown
And is maturing into an adult
Feeling inadequate to fill the
Mold that society has set as the example.
When you feel a little bit scared
Look inside
There's the child you yearn to be
It's inside you.
Look forward to the future
And know that you can always keep the
Memories.**

As Suddenly As We Began
We were over as suddenly as
We began
And there was nothing
I could do about it.
I didn't want us to
Be over so soon,
But you nor I could
Help the end slow down.
Time will tell how
Strong our feelings
For each other were
And we are over
As suddenly as we began.

Grow Up
You are so immature in
Everything you do.
You should have learned
A long time ago
The difference between
Right and wrong.
All I have to tell
You is: Grow up
You're so immature.
You need to get a higher
Level of maturity
You act like such a baby
You're not a baby anymore
I hate to break that to you.
So now that I have
Grow up.

Even More Confused
Now I am even more confused than I was before.
I realize that it is easy to confuse me.
But, I was so over you
I moved on with my life and
Now you're back again.
You wait to talk to me,
You write me often,
I just can't believe
That now I have gotten my life back on track
You've reentered into my life
And caused me more heartache.
I can't stop thinking about you,
But when I close my eyes all I can picture
Is the hurt on his face.
I don't want to hurt him,
I don't want to choose.
I made my choice a long time ago when
You said, "I don't like you, I like her."
Why does life have to be so confusing?
I try to take it day by day
But since you said that you and she were over
You kept talking to me more.
I told you before,
I'm not one to hurt
I couldn't ever hurt you
As you have hurt me.
Your words scarred me deeply
And I have moved on with his help
Not yours.
Yes once I did like you
Now I'm not so sure
All I know is that I'm even more confused
Than when I started.

Even More Confused

When things become complicated
You run to me
I cannot help you
I'm even more confused.

Not A Man

You are not a man.
You are nothing that I thought
You were.
I thought the world of you.
Yes it's true I
View the world with rose-colored glasses.
I felt it was better that way.
A man would have told me what was going on
And he would have been up-front with me.
You know how I hate lying
Which is what you did.
You lied not only to me but to
Your parents.
I feel bad for them.
A man would have been straight up
To everyone about what was happening.

Pissed Off - Pissed On

My father always says,
" It's better to be pissed off than to be pissed on."
I feel that I have been pissed on by you.
You have robbed me of my thinking
I don't know what to believe.
You have me so confused.
I think you pissed on me and
I hate you for it.
So understand that I am so
Pissed off at you.
I wouldn't care if you lived
Or died.
Life sucks it's true.
So piss people off and get
Pissed on.

I’m Letting You Go

There is a noise that breaks
The stillness of the room.
Fear not it’s just my heart
Cracking with the sorrow
Of the loss of you.
I’m broken hearted
Yes it’s true
I love you.
I know that you don’t love me anymore.
And time will heal my heart
Slowly - ever so slowly
I am letting you go.
I’m allowing myself to
Learn to love again
And I’m teaching myself
To trust again.
I’m slowly letting you go
And moving on with
My life.
It’s so hard for me to let
You go and that’s
Because I still love
You and I always will
Slowly but surely
I’m letting you go.

Fighter

Look whose heart you're holding
You're holding my heart in your hands.
Your grip gets tighter every second
And I yearn to break free.
Yet your grip gains strength
And I become weaker
You prey upon girls
And I'm one girl that will never
Give into you - ever.
I fight back
And once I am free
Others will be warned about you.
For this is my fight
All my strength must go in it
You may think me weak
I'm not weak - I'm a fighter.
Never losing faith
If it takes me eternity
I'll free myself from you.

Tearing My Insides Out

**I don't know if I did the right thing
My mother always told me to follow my heart.
I couldn't tell you all I feel inside.
I'm not the best speaker
I can't express myself vocally
Words written down is
The best way for me to express myself.
I'm tearing myself apart inside over you.
I love you - I hate you.
I don't know what I feel.
I believe I have the right to feel hurt
And the right to feel I was lied to.
Trust is gained over time
I should've learned that
Instead I jumped to the fact that I
Automatically trusted you.
Now I have learned for next time.
When I was telling you how I felt
I didn't want to hear you reaction
But I knew it was inevitable.
You are probably mad at me
And you have no right to be.
You screwed me over royally.
Yet though all you did was
Hurt me
I still care for you.
I'm probably a fool
But I'm tearing myself apart over you.**

Until Later

Maybe I disagree with you
And your actions.
But I'm not at liberty to say
What's wrong and right.
I think you made
The wrong choice in
Letting me go.
But now I have my freedom
And I'm not giving it up so
Easily.
I gave it up once
For you and
You stole my trust
And now I want it back.
It's so hard to say goodbye
To you because of things
We shared.
Those things will be implanted in my
Heart forever.
I will forever be a part of you
As you will be me
And those times we shared
Can never be relived.
We will only say goodbye
For now
Since I will see you
In eternity.

Forgotten / Adieu

Forgotten
I'm just a grain of sand on the beach.
I'm just a pebble among the rocks.
I'm just one of your ex' es.
As soon as we are over
I'll be forgotten.
I meant something to you for a
Short while that seems so long ago.
I never hurt you - you screwed yourself
With the mind games you played.
All I want to be is forgotten.
I will never forget the time we
Spent together, but to you
I'll be forgotten.

Adieu
This is my farewell to you.
I think you should know
That I'm not coming back.
This is my goodbye to
You, who left me for her.
I don't need you
By my side,
I'm better off on my own
So no matter how
It is said:
Goodbye,
Adios,
They all mean the same thing:
I'm leaving and
Not coming back
So this is my way of
Saying adieu.

Why Did You Do This To Me?

Why did you do this to me?
Do you derive a great pleasure from
Hurting other people?
Did you think about it before
You made a choice?
Did you think of the consequences
Of you choice?
You didn't think that
I'd find out did you?
I don't understand why you would
Do this to me -
I thought you loved me.
You don't do you?
Was that just a trick to
Get more from me than I'd give?
This is the way I feel
I don't know your reasons
So go.

Screaming

Shouting at the top of
My lungs,
My head held toward the sky
Screaming curses at the stars.
Why me?
What did I do to deserve this?
No one can hear me
I'm reaching out to someone
To anyone
Can't anyone hear my screams
Of agony?
Of torture?
My mind must be playing tricks
On me again.
It must have fooled me into believing
That I was worth something.
I'm screaming with the pain of
A love lost and never be forgotten.

Without You In My Arms

I need to feel you in my arms.
At night when you're at your home
My arms feel empty.
I miss you so much at night
More than you could ever know.
I can't wait until the next morning
When I see you again.
With out you in my arms
I feel so alone and empty.
I pass the hours of the night by
Dreaming of you and me,
I dream that you hold me close and
Will never let me go until we have
To go home.
I guess that it is good
That we don't see
Each other twenty - four seven.
That way we have our own space.
I don't want my space from you
I need to hold you in my arms.
Without you in my arms I
Feel so alone.
So I hold the memories
Of that day
Close at night
And I wait until morning
When I see you again.

Reverse Psychology

Relationships are built on trust.
I do have trust in you.
Why is it that when I talk to you
You are so sweet and
Then it's like you barely notice
I'm alive?
I know it's nothing I do
So in order for you to like me
As I like you
A little reverse psychology
Is the doctor's prescription.
A little reverse psychology never hurt
Anyone so why should it hurt you?
Your heart may not be capable of love
And I have to find out.
The next time we meet
Some reverse psychology
Will be used and
We'll see how you like your
Games being played
Back at you.
I'm good at them
I play by the rules
And no matter what
You do
I'll win.

Free

I've had my taste of freedom
And I like it.
I don't think I deserve to be
Trapped in the cage of your
Love for the rest of my life
We are so young
And I want to be free.
I want to fly away from my
Troubles and sorrows
Like the birds in flight.
They can up and leave when
They so desire.
I can't yet I want that opportunity.
You have no right to cage me like
An animal I am
A human with feelings
And I need my freedom to
Grow as a person.
Let me leave now
And we'll both be better
Off later.

Mind Games

**I don't know what you're trying to do.
One time it's all, "I love you,"
The next you're ignoring me.
You are sending me mixed signals
And you're messing with my head.
I don't need my head messed with.
I'm good enough only sometimes
I think not.
Don't think you can play these
Games and get away with it.
I won't tolerate it.
You'll see I'll play
By your rules
And I'll win anyway.
You won't know what hit you
You're in for a fall
Higher than the tallest building
And you'll fall faster than lighting.
You'll see what a mistake it was to play with
My head
I can play the game too
Don't think I can't.
I'll play by the rules you set
Win anyway.**

Tired of Lies

**I'm so tired.
I'm tired of lies, of love, of parts of life.
Why can't we begin our lives at the end
And work our way back to the beginning?
Life would be less complicated that
Way don't you think?
I'm tired of believing that
Something will happen that is
Just a dream that can never
Become reality.
I'm tired of not knowing
What life will bring
Complications are supposed
To make us stronger
But I don't see how they are
Helping me grow into
A more mature person.
I'm tired of being lied to.
The last time someone lied to me
I said goodbye.**

Never Hurt You

Your past is yours
It can never be taken back or replaced
As we grow older together
You must come to realize
That I'll cause you no pain
In your life
Only joy will be yours.
Past relationships
Have left you (and I)
With a sense of
There is something more
To be found
Finally seeing that they're not the one.
First time meeting you
Already knowing by
Reading your past in your eyes
Seeing pain and betrayal
Know I shall never hurt you.
In time you will begin to trust
Me more - for now
Fingertip to fingertip
Eyes locked on eyes
As I mutter these words:
"Never could I hurt you"
You begin to believe me
Slowly at first
With the eyes of a child
You whisper,
"Always?"
A moments pause
Lifting my head
I reply:

“Always.”

www.ingramcontent.com/pod-product-compliance
Ingram Content Group UK Ltd.
Pitfield, Milton Keynes, MK11 3LW, UK
UKHW040601210726
13854UKWH00008B/1704

9 781411 60366